NASA'S ARTEMIS MISSIONS

NASA'S ARTEMIS MISSIONS

EXPLORING the MOON

Ben Hubbard

LERNER PUBLICATIONS ◆ MINNEAPOLIS

For Geoff and Sheila

Lerner Publications Company
An imprint of Lerner Publishing Group, Inc.
241 First Avenue North
Minneapolis, MN 55401 USA

For reading levels and more information, look up this title at www.lernerbooks.com.

Main body text set in ITC Garamond Std Book.
Typeface provided by Adobe Systems.

Designer: Athena Currier

Library of Congress Cataloging-in-Publication Data

Names: Hubbard, Ben, 1973– author
Title: NASAs Artemis missions : exploring the moon / Ben Hubbard.
Other titles: National Aeronautics and Space Administration's Artemis missions
Description: Minneapolis : Lerner Publications, [2026] | Series: Gateway headlines | Includes bibliographical references and index. | Audience term: juvenile | Audience: Ages 9–14 Lerner Publications | Audience: Grades 4–6 Lerner Publications | Summary: "NASA's Artemis missions aim to explore the Moon and build on it. Readers discover the history and future of the Artemis missions, including plans, logistical issues, and concerns for the missions' goals"— Provided by publisher.
Identifiers: LCCN 2024045860 (print) | LCCN 2024045861 (ebook) | ISBN 9798765669389 library binding | ISBN 9798765684139 paperback | ISBN 9798765677575 epub
Subjects: LCSH: Artemis Program (U.S.)—Juvenile literature | Space flight to the moon—Juvenile literature | Moon—Exploration—Juvenile literature
Classification: LCC TL799.M6 H78 2026 (print) | LCC TL799.M6 (ebook) | DDC 629.45/4—dc23/eng/20250131

LC record available at https://lccn.loc.gov/2024045860
LC ebook record available at https://lccn.loc.gov/2024045861

Manufactured in the United States of America
1-1011880-53909-3/6/2025

Table of Contents

Starship prepares to launch on November 18, 2023.

On November 18, 2023, a powerful rocket prepared to blast into space. Spectators gathered to watch the forty-story-high rocket lift off from its launchpad in Boca Chica, Texas. Viewers across the globe tuned into the live feed on their computer screens. Everyone was excited to be a part of this historic moment in modern space development.

The rocket—called Starship—was designed by the private space company SpaceX for an important mission: to send humans to the Moon and maybe one day to Mars. But during this launch, no one was on board the Starship. Instead, the uncrewed test flight was planned to fly into space, orbit Earth, and splash down into the Pacific Ocean near Hawaii. Would it succeed in its mission?

The countdown from the Boca Chica operations center began. All eyes watched as Starship rumbled to life. Red-and-orange flames sparked upward as white exhaust smoke blew out from the rocket's engines and billowed along the ground. The operations crew cheered as the rocket shook, rocked, and rose slowly into the air.

After two minutes, the rocket began its first maneuver. The bottom part of the rocket, called a booster, separated from Starship. The booster was supposed to splash down into the Gulf of Mexico, but then its engines shut down. There were gasps as the booster unexpectedly exploded.

Meanwhile, the rest of Starship was still flying toward space. The rocket was traveling at 15,000 miles (24,000 km) per hour and had reached an altitude of

Flames trail behind Starship as it launches on November 18, 2023.

91 miles (147 km). But there was no more cheering at the operations center. Communication with the rocket had been lost. Everyone watched with concern. Suddenly, the rocket's automatic termination was triggered. Starship exploded above the sea. The test flight was over.

A rocket exploding in space is a scary idea—especially if astronauts are on board. People worried because Starship had been picked by the National Aeronautics and Space Administration (NASA) to deliver astronauts to the Moon as part of its bold new Artemis program. Made up of six main missions that will fly astronauts around the Moon, Artemis will create a space station in the Moon's low orbit and land the first humans on the lunar surface in over fifty years. Then the Artemis program will build a permanent base on the Moon to prepare astronauts for the first crewed missions to Mars.

To achieve all these highly ambitious and expensive goals, NASA signed contracts with private space companies, including SpaceX and Blue Origin, to build some of the rockets. But back in November 2023, SpaceX's rocket development did not seem to be going well. Surely, Starship exploding in midair was a major disaster, right?

Not according to the experts. Rockets exploding, crashing, or even failing to launch is part of their development. These events have been happening since the dawn of space rocket technology in the 1950s. Starship exploding was considered not a failure but a success. "That's why we test, you know. You learn more from a test that doesn't go well than from one that does go well, and then you regroup and go again," said Lisa Watson-Morgan, the program manager for NASA's Human Landing System.

Lonely Moon

Artemis plans to put people on the Moon again. Humans have not been to the Moon since the US government canceled its Apollo program in 1972. Apollo consisted of eleven crewed Moon missions between 1969 and 1972, including six lunar landings. The Apollo program, named after Greek and Roman god Apollo, marked the greatest space accomplishment in history. The Artemis missions—named after Apollo's twin sister, the Greek goddess Artemis—hope to reignite human interest in space.

Apollo 7, the first of the Apollo missions to reach space, launches in October 1968.

The Apollo program was part of a competition called the space race between the United States and the Soviet Union (USSR). The USSR, a union of fifteen republics including Russia, collapsed in 1991 and was an enemy of the US. The rival countries wanted to prove that they each had the best rocket technology.

The USSR won the first round by launching a satellite into space in 1957. This stunned US scientists, who had not yet designed a powerful enough rocket to reach space. Then the USSR struck another blow in 1961 by launching the first person, Yuri Gagarin, into space aboard the Vostok 1 spacecraft. This showed the US was again behind the USSR.

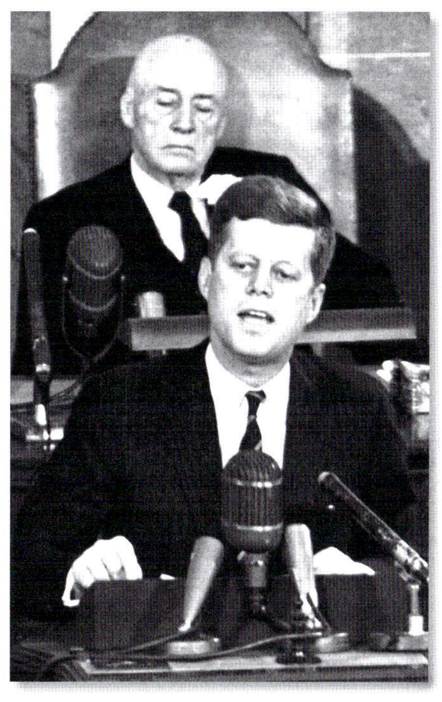

On May 25, 1961, President John F. Kennedy announces his goal for the US to put humans on the Moon.

To catch up, US President John F. Kennedy made a huge announcement in 1961. He said the US would "commit itself to achieving the goal, before this decade is out, of landing a man on the Moon and returning him safely to the Earth." Kennedy's speech surprised everyone, including NASA's scientists, who had not even sent an astronaut into space. To land people on the Moon meant building a rocket powerful enough to blast off from Earth, reach the Moon, and then travel safely back. There was little time to achieve this huge task.

As the clock ticked, corners were cut, and several tragic incidents occurred. In 1967 Apollo astronauts Edward White, Virgil Grissom, and Roger Chaffee were testing their Apollo command capsule when a fire broke out and killed all three astronauts. In 1968 the Saturn V rocket designed to carry astronauts to the Moon failed to launch and shook on its own launchpad. Shortly after, the Soviet Union's thirty-engine N1 rocket blew up, causing one of the largest explosions in space history.

Despite the space race failures and tragedies, Apollo 11 became the first mission to land astronauts on the Moon in July 1969. Neil Armstrong was the first human to step onto the lunar surface and utter some immortal words as he did so: "That's one small step for man, one giant leap for mankind."

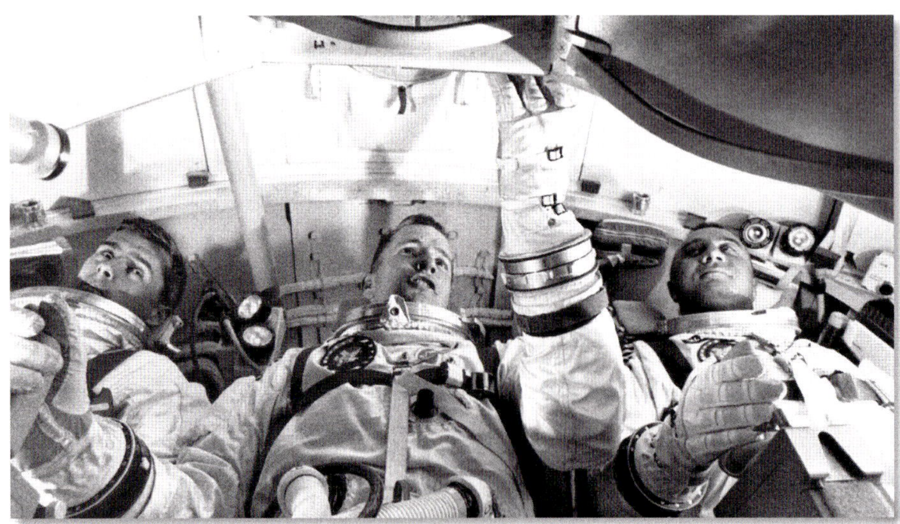

Left to right: ***Astronauts Roger Chaffee, Edward White, and Virgil Grissom died during a practice test of their command module on January 27, 1967.***

Astronaut Buzz Aldrin on the Moon during the Apollo 11 mission in 1969

The Moon landing meant the US had won the space race, but the Apollo program would not last. One of the main problems was money. The Apollo program had cost about $26 billion, or more than $200 billion in modern currency. This was a massive sum. Apollo 17 in 1972 became the final mission before the program was canceled. The Moon has remained without visitors ever since.

THE INTERNATIONAL SPACE STATION

The International Space Station (ISS) was built in Earth's low orbit starting in 1998. Fifteen countries, including the US and Russia, contributed modules until the ISS was the size of a football field. A module is a small, self-contained unit that can be a living space, laboratory, storage, and more.

Astronauts from around the world have stayed on the ISS for months at a time to conduct experiments and learn about the effects of living in space. The Russian Soyuz spacecraft and US space shuttles originally provided transport to and from the ISS. Starting in 2011, SpaceX's Dragon spacecraft were also used. For the first time a private company was hired by NASA to provide space transportation.

Artemis Begins

In 2010 US President Barack Obama announced funding for NASA to create a new space program. "By the mid-2030s, I believe we can send humans to orbit Mars and return them safely to Earth," Obama said. Included in the $58 billion package was $3 billion to design a new heavy-lift rocket called the Space Launch System (SLS).

In 2017 plans for the new space program were stepped up with the Space Policy Directive 1. The directive allowed NASA to work with private companies for its new space program, which soon had a name: Artemis. Then NASA revealed the details behind Artemis.

The Space Launch System and Orion spacecraft undergo a rehearsal at the Kennedy Space Center in 2022.

Artemis's primary aim was ambitious but simple: Fly humans to the Moon so they could learn to live on another world. This would prepare people for later crewed missions to Mars.

Traveling to the Moon would occur over the first six Artemis missions. The first of these, Artemis 1, launched the SLS from NASA's Kennedy Space Center to the Moon. Without a crew, it orbited the Moon once and returned to Earth. Atop the SLS sat Orion, the spacecraft that would later carry astronauts.

Artemis 2 plans to fly astronauts Reid Wiseman, Victor Glover, Christina Koch, and Jeremy Hansen around the Moon and back to Earth. The mission will be the first time a woman, a person of color, and a non-American will travel beyond Earth's low orbit.

Left to right: ***Astronauts Reid Wiseman, Victor Glover, Christina Koch, and Jeremy Hansen at a press conference in 2023***

Artemis 3 will send four astronauts to the Moon's low orbit. There, the Orion spacecraft will dock with the Starship Human Landing System (HLS), a lunar lander sent from Earth sometime earlier. The HLS will then land two astronauts at the lunar south pole, while two other astronauts remain aboard Orion in the Moon's orbit. After a week, the HLS will fly the lunar astronauts to redock with Orion. Orion will then fly all four astronauts back to Earth.

Artemis 4 will have the same goals as Artemis 3 but will also bring a new module with it. This would be added to the previous module to become a new space station, called Gateway. Located in the Moon's low orbit, Gateway will act as a place for astronauts to stay between landings to the lunar surface. Artemis 4 will conduct such a lunar mission aboard the HLS, before redocking with Orion and flying home.

Artemis 5 and 6 will be similar missions to Artemis 4. They will add modules to Gateway and conduct lunar landings. During these landings, the astronauts will fly a new Blue Origin lunar lander to the south pole and deliver hardware, including a lunar terrain vehicle.

The Artemis program represents the first time humans will land on the Moon's south pole. This pole is the proposed site for a future Moon base. This is because robotic craft orbiting the Moon in 1998 first detected water ice in its deep polar craters. Water is essential for human survival, so it makes sense for the first base on another world to be built near it.

WHY THE MOON?

At about 239,000 miles (384,630 km) from Earth, the Moon is the closest world to us. But it is also a barren wasteland with no atmosphere, oxygen, or life. The Moon has large swings in temperature, from as cold as −410°F (−246°C) to as hot as 250°F (121°C). And its surface is marked by craters and covered in a fine gray dust. So why would humans go there? The main reason is to test living on another world and prepare humans to travel to Mars. The Moon's water ice can be separated into two chemical components—oxygen to breathe and hydrogen to make rocket fuel. The Moon also contains valuable resources such as iron, titanium, and uranium to be mined.

The Copernicus crater on the Moon is 58 miles (93 km) wide.

Space Partnerships

Creating the most ambitious space program in history is costly. According to NASA, the Artemis program will cost about $93 billion between 2017 and 2025. Each of the first four Artemis SLS launches will cost about $4.2 billion. This is why during Artemis, unlike the earlier Apollo program, NASA decided to contract some of the work to private companies.

For the first time, organizations other than NASA would supply the rockets and hardware needed to get astronauts to the Moon. By splitting the cost of the Artemis missions, the US government would be able to afford its ambitious space plans. It would also enable private companies such as SpaceX, Blue Origin, and

Space Exploration Technologies Corporation, known as SpaceX, was created in 2002 by Elon Musk.

Boeing to learn how to build new and better rockets while being paid as contractors for the US government.

Space, for these companies, represents a new, untapped way of making money. Companies taking paying customers into space for a few hours is increasingly common and highly profitable. Space tourism may become a mainstream activity over the next decade. There are even plans for hotels in Earth's low orbit. Space could be big business.

"What I think we're beginning to see is the dawn of a new era of space exploration. One that is driven by commercial companies as much, if not more, than by government," SpaceX founder Elon Musk said in 2004.

Around sixty tourists have gone to space. Dennis Tito was the first space tourist in 2001.

SPACE ROCKETS

To reach the required roughly 25,000 miles (40,200 km) per hour speed to break away from Earth's gravitational pull and reach the Moon, a multistage rocket must be used. As each stage burns through its fuel, it falls away to reveal another stage above it. At 322 feet (98 m) tall, the SLS is NASA's most powerful multistage rocket.

SpaceX's Starship is even taller than the SLS, at 397 feet (121 m). It is also a reusable rocket. Scientists hope that Starship can one day take humans to and from Mars. The Starship being used in the Artemis 3 mission will only fly astronauts from the Moon's orbit to its surface and back.

SpaceX's Starship rocket in 2024

Making the Artemis partnership between private companies and NASA a success has sometimes proved difficult. Choosing a company to work with is often a task all its own. In 2020 NASA provided funding to the companies SpaceX, Blue Origin, and Dynetics to develop a lunar lander that would land Artemis 3 astronauts on the Moon. In 2021 NASA announced SpaceX's Starship Human Landing System had won the $2.9 billion contract—but Blue Origin and Dynetics protested. Blue Origin even took NASA to court over its decision, claiming safety issues to do with Starship. A judge dismissed the case after months of arguments.

Then, in 2022, NASA surprised everyone by announcing it wanted a second lunar lander, likely for the Artemis 5 mission, to be built by a different company. Despite its lawsuit against NASA, Blue Origin won the contract with its Blue Origin lunar lander. In explaining the move, NASA said that it encouraged competition among its contractors to drive innovation and reduce costs. "We are in a golden age of human spaceflight, which is made possible by NASA's commercial and international partnerships," NASA administrator Bill Nelson explained. So, while SpaceX and Blue Origin went to work to provide systems for the later Artemis missions, all eyes turned to the mission at hand: Artemis 1.

Artemis 1 Prepares

Artemis 1 had a lot riding on it. It was the first time an SLS carrying the Orion spacecraft would blast off to the Moon. It was also the first time Orion would fly by the Moon and back to Earth. But above all else, it would be the first test of Orion's heat shield, needed to safely reenter Earth's atmosphere.

Avcoat tiles on Orion's head shield

During reentry, a spacecraft enters Earth's atmosphere at about 25,000 miles (40,200 km) per hour. It then hits pockets of air, which cause friction and intense temperatures of 5,000°F (2,760°C). To stop the spacecraft from burning up, a heat shield is built in. On Orion, this heat shield is made of Avcoat tiles, which direct heat away from the spacecraft. This heat shield was tested more than one thousand times on Earth, but the only true test would be during reentry. The Artemis 1 Orion spacecraft was uncrewed but had mannequins in place of the astronauts. Nobody at NASA wanted to see these mannequins melt or burn because of a faulty heat shield.

Preparations for Artemis 1 intensified in April 2021 with the stacking of the SLS in the Vehicle Assembly Building in Florida. Stacking is putting one rocket stage on top of the other like building blocks, starting with the core stage. Providing over 2 million pounds (0.9 million kg) of thrust to get the SLS off the ground, the core stage was 212 feet (65 m) tall and had four engines to burn over 733,000 gallons (2,774,707 L) of liquid fuel. After the other stages were added to the SLS, Orion was fitted to the top of the SLS. With the stacking complete, the SLS was rolled out to its launchpad. It traveled 4 miles (6 km), taking over ten hours.

The Space Launch System and Orion spacecraft are assembled in the Vehicle Assembly Building at the Kennedy Space Center.

When Artemis 1 finally stood on its launchpad, there was a problem. The first test of the rocket's engines, called a wet dress rehearsal, had to be canceled. Engineers found an issue with the rocket's launch system. After this was fixed, a faulty valve was detected before the second wet dress rehearsal. Then, before the third wet rehearsal, more technical problems were discovered. During the fourth wet rehearsal, the launch went into the countdown and had only twenty-nine seconds to go before a hydrogen leak shut down the rocket automatically.

To address each issue, the SLS had to be rolled back to the Vehicle Assembly Building to fix the problem. This meant a schedule delay of several months. On August 29, 2022, Artemis was rolled to its launchpad. People thought this was the date NASA would make history. They were wrong. An offshore storm delayed the launch, and then one of the engines had a fuel leak. The launch was again canceled. Another fuel leak caused a further cancelation on September 3. New launch dates of September 27 and November 14 also had to be canceled. Would Artemis 1 ever get off the ground?

The delays were disappointing but simply a part of launching the most complex rocket ever constructed, according to NASA administrator Bill Nelson: "We don't launch until it's right. . . . [This] is a very complicated machine, a very complicated system, and all those things have to work. You don't light the candle until it's ready to go."

On November 16, Artemis 1 was rolled out again to its launchpad. A signed banner by NASA workers on the fence next to the launchpad read: "We are going!" Staff

The Artemis 1 rocket on its launchpad on November 16, 2022

at NASA's operations center got into position. People crossed their fingers as the countdown for Artemis 1 commenced.

Artemis 1 Liftoff

At just after one in the morning on November 16, 2022, Artemis 1 finally blasted off from its launchpad at the Kennedy Space Center in Florida. The operations crew whooped in delight. Then they watched intently. If anything was going to go wrong, it was likely to occur within the first few minutes.

The Artemis 1 rocket blasts off on November 16, 2022.

After two minutes, the SLS shed its booster rockets as it reached a speed of over 3,000 miles (4,828 km) per hour. The rocket was experiencing intense pressure on its hull. But Artemis continued to rise steadily. After three minutes, the SLS shed its launch abort system. This was a last chance for Orion to abort and fly away from the rocket in an emergency. After eight minutes, the SLS shed its core stage as it reached space.

Leaving Earth was a big first step, but the hard part of the journey was still to come. Artemis 1 now consisted of two parts: an interim cryogenic propulsion stage and the Orion spacecraft. After one hour and thirty-six minutes, Artemis's engines fired to bring it up to a speed of 22,600 miles (36,371 km) per hour so it could leave Earth's orbit. It then shed the cryogenic propulsion stage and ten small satellites called CubeSats.

Only the Orion spacecraft was left to fly to the Moon. On November 28 the spacecraft flew into the Moon's orbit. Before long, it had traveled around the Moon into its dark side, out of sight of Earth. At this time, Orion reached about 270,000 miles (434,520 km) away from Earth—the farthest a spacecraft designed to transport people has ever traveled.

Finally, Orion began its journey home. Apart from one minor electrical issue, which was fixed, the mission had so far been a success. But the difficult reentry was coming up. Would the all-important heat shield hold? This was a vital test because the next Orion splashing down to Earth would not be carrying mannequins but astronauts.

On December 11, Orion reentered Earth's atmosphere at 25,000 miles (40,234 km) per hour after twenty-five days in space. As it sped toward its splashdown point in the Pacific Ocean, Orion became a fireball that left a blazing trail behind it. Then, to the shock of NASA engineers, pieces of charred heat shield began flying off Orion. Despite this, the spacecraft splashed down into the water. It was then retrieved by the US Navy. The mannequins inside were intact and unharmed. Artemis 1 was over.

ORION

Orion is the spacecraft that will transport the Artemis astronauts and act as their base while in the Moon's orbit. Built of aluminium sheets and thermal protection to keep the astronauts both warm and cool, Orion is a small home away from home. It contains enough power, oxygen, food, and water for four astronauts for twenty-one days. There is one compact toilet and an exercise machine to keep the astronauts fit. The astronauts will sleep by attaching their sleeping bags to an inside wall of Orion.

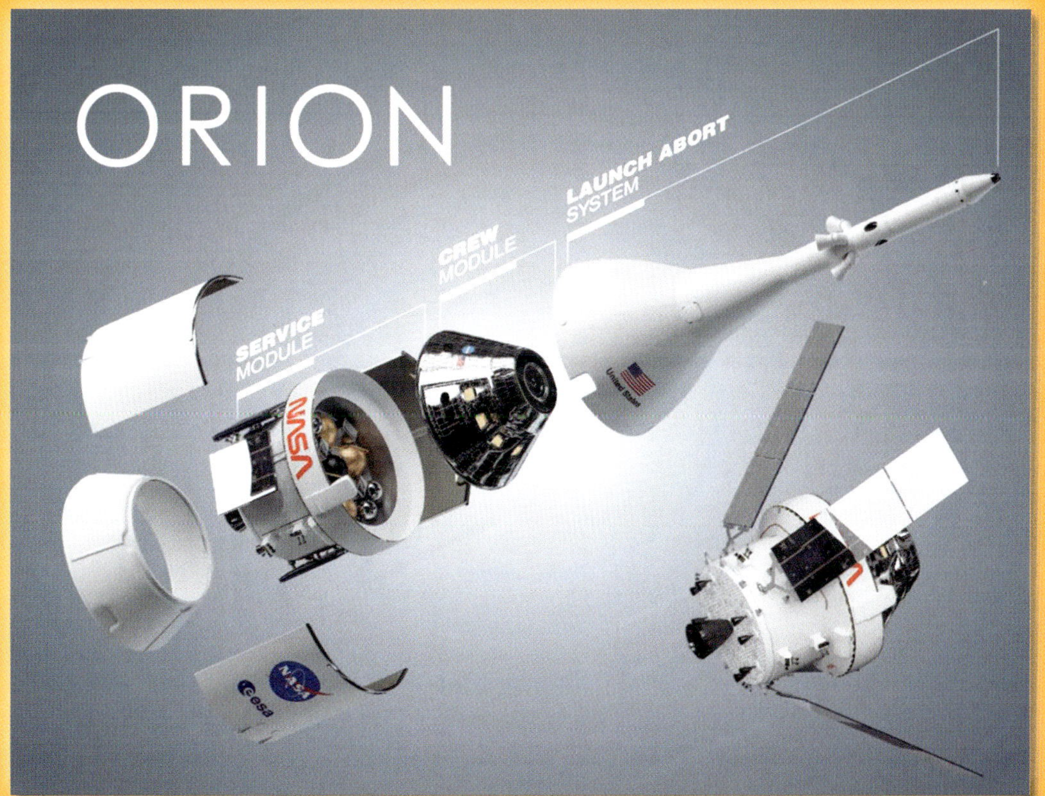

Artemis 2 Delays

After the success of Artemis 1, the Artemis 2 mission took center stage. The first mission to fly humans to the Moon in over fifty years had been scheduled for 2024. But news of the failed heat shield on Artemis 1 concerned NASA administrators. A NASA investigation report of the Artemis 1 Orion spacecraft showed that "the test flight revealed [issues] with the Orion heat shield, separation bolts, and power distribution that pose significant risk to the safety of the crew."

Damage to the Orion spacecraft's heat shield after the Artemis 1 test flight

The heat shield had not performed as expected and was worn away in more than one hundred different places. This was a serious issue that could put the lives of the astronauts at risk. In January 2024 NASA announced the launch of Artemis 2 would be delayed until late 2025. But some experts say 2026 is more likely. Nothing is certain in the scheduling of space missions.

Astronaut safety during Artemis 2 is the highest priority. Having a reliable heat shield to prevent Orion burning up on reentry is essential. For the Artemis 2 astronauts, the delay caused by the damaged Artemis 1 heat shield was disappointing but understandable. "We look at many risks, but when you have learned something that you didn't know—and you realize there's something that you can do about it and to learn more—it just makes sense to delay," said Artemis 2 astronaut Jeremy Hansen.

Meanwhile, the astronauts had a lot to do. Their mission training included practicing how to live and work in an Orion spacecraft simulator. Around the size of two minivans, Orion would be the astronauts' home for the ten-day mission to perform flybys of Earth and the Moon. But the four astronauts would also have to eat, sleep, wash, and use the bathroom in a small capsule with no gravity on board to hold them down.

Once in space, the Artemis 2 astronauts—Reid Wiseman, Victor Glover, Christina Koch, and Jeremy Hansen—will also have to fix any issues that arise. Since these may include technical problems with Orion,

This Orion spacecraft simulator helps astronauts train for the Artemis 2 mission.

the astronauts trained to understand every inch of the spacecraft. If a fuel or oxygen leak occurred, or Orion got hit by flying space debris, the astronauts would have to fix it. No one could come to help them that far away from Earth.

If all else fails, the astronauts will be able to rely on their space suits, called Orion Crew Survival Systems. The suits are fitted with thermal material and cooling tubes to keep the astronauts at the right temperature. The helmets contain communications systems and oxygen tubes so the astronauts can survive if the air supply fails in Orion. The suits are also bright orange so the astronauts can be easily found if they get stranded at sea after splashdown. The astronauts also perform activities in the suits as part of their training.

The astronauts will have to eat in space too, and there is no gravity to keep food on plates. So, what's on the menu? The Artemis 2 meals will include maple cream cookies, smoked salmon, shrimp curry with rice, and strawberry-lavender cereal. Each meal is individually wrapped in plastic, ready to be warmed up or have hot water added. Learning to eat this space food is another part of the training the Artemis astronauts undergo in the Orion spacecraft simulator.

Left to right: ***Artemis 2 astronauts Jeremy Hansen, Christina Koch, Victor Glover, and Reid Wiseman practice for their mission launch.***

Artemis 3 Concerns

The January 2024 news that Artemis 2 had been delayed disappointed many people. It followed bad news about Artemis 3 in November 2023. During a test flight of SpaceX's Starship, the rocket had exploded minutes after liftoff. The Artemis 3 schedule was at risk. Would SpaceX be able to meet its responsibilities under its NASA contract?

Starship is the rocket planned to transport astronauts to and from the lunar surface. But one Starship cannot fly directly to the Moon. Instead, several Starship rockets will be used. One will sit in Earth's low orbit as a fueling station. This will refuel the Starship that flies to the Moon to act as the HLS.

The astronauts launching from Earth aboard Orion will dock with the Starship HLS in the Moon's orbit. Two astronauts will then fly to and from the lunar south pole aboard the HLS, while the other two stay aboard Orion. Because the HLS will stay in space, it will not need the Earth reentry heat shield, which caused the problems on Artemis 2. But SpaceX needed to prove Starship would not blow up—especially with astronauts on board.

SpaceX's NASA contract required that an uncrewed Starship HLS could land safely on the Moon before the Artemis 3 mission began. But the exploded Starship would delay this objective. During a media conference in January 2024, a SpaceX spokesperson said a Starship HLS would hopefully land on the Moon sometime in 2025. NASA officials then announced that the Artemis

3 mission would be delayed until September 2026. This new Artemis 3 delay brought more disappointment and annoyed some US politicians. They worried that rival countries might beat the US to the Moon, which could cause conflict in space.

"It's no secret that China has a goal to surpass the United States by 2045 as global leaders in space. We can't allow this to happen. I think the leading edge that we have in space technology will protect the United States—not just the economy, but technologies that can benefit humankind," said US House of Representatives' Committee on Science, Space, and Technology member Rich McCormick.

Concept art of the Starship Human Landing System on the Moon

GATEWAY

Gateway is a space station to be built by NASA and international partners in the Moon's low orbit. There, it will connect the Moon and Earth. Astronauts traveling from Earth will dock at Gateway before taking a lander to the lunar surface. They will then redock with Gateway before heading back to Earth. Gateway will have research facilities, living quarters, and cargo areas for supplies. Like the ISS, Gateway will be made up of different modules and assembled over several years. If successful, Gateway will later serve as a stopping-off point between Earth and crewed missions to Mars.

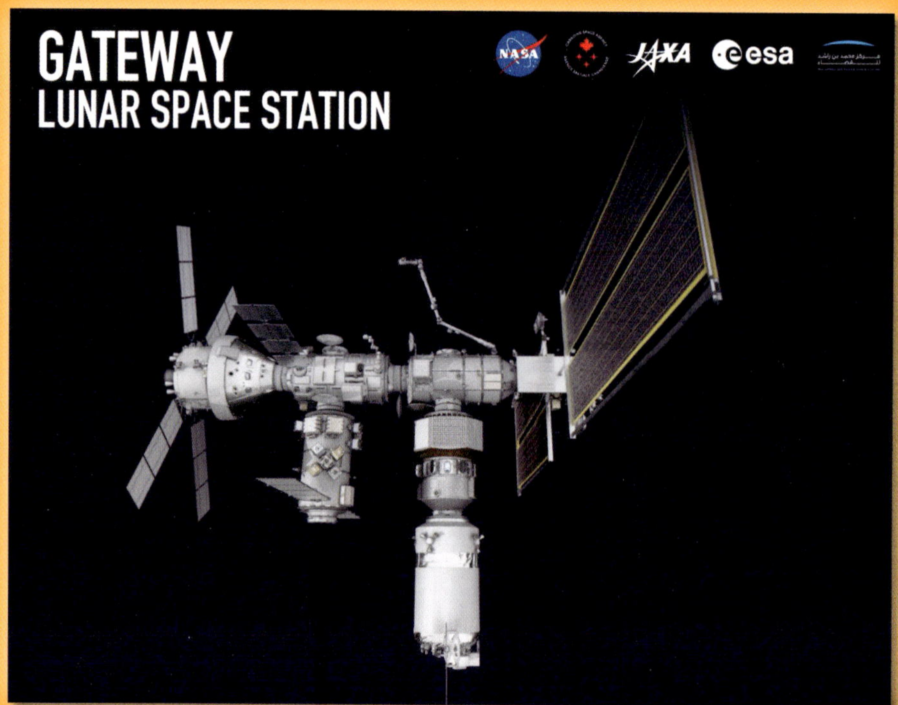

To address the politicians' concerns, NASA stepped up its Moon efforts. It asked SpaceX and Blue Origin to start developing rockets to transport cargo to the Moon. This is a vital part of the Artemis 3 mission. Astronauts will have the equipment to make geological surveys and retrieve samples to be studied back on Earth. As they perform these tasks, the astronauts will send back pictures and videos for the world to see. Then, after a week, the astronauts will fly the HLS to redock with Orion. Finally, the four astronauts will spend up to five days in lunar orbit transferring samples from the HLS and preparing for the journey back to Earth. Once completed, the thirty-day mission will have achieved one of the Artemis program's main objectives—to work and live on the Moon.

Moon Base and Beyond

On March 14, 2024, SpaceX reported some good news. The third test flight of Starship had been a success. The rocket fired all its thirty-three engines and separated from its stages before reaching space and flying once around Earth. The only issue occurred during the rocket's reentry, when it was lost and probably exploded. But the launch brought Artemis 3 one step closer to reality.

Meanwhile, planning is underway for Artemis 4, 5, and 6, scheduled for 2028, 2030, and 2031, respectively. These missions will combine crewed exploration of the

Starship's third test flight launches on March 14, 2024.

lunar surface with construction of Gateway. Robotic landers, rovers, scientific equipment, and building materials will be transported by private companies to the lunar south pole aboard uncrewed rockets. The materials will be used in the construction of a Moon base, called the Artemis Base Camp.

The first module of the base camp is called the Surface Habitat. It will be three stories high, with a metal basement air lock and two inflatable floors above. These floors will contain life-support equipment such as oxygen and water, private crew quarters, a kitchen, exercise equipment, a bathroom, a medical bay, and a laboratory for scientific experiments. The Surface Habitat will recycle air and water and be able to support two astronauts for thirty days at a time. Like Gateway, more modules will be added to the Artemis Base Camp over time, which will allow for longer stays for more astronauts.

During their lunar visits, astronauts will collect Moon rock samples, explore the area around the south pole for water ice, and study how the human body copes with living on the Moon. The Moon has a sixth of the gravity on Earth, which can cause bloating and muscle loss.

Bigelow Aerospace is one company that creates inflatable habitats for use in space.

A permanent Moon base is one long-term goal of the Artemis program. But after Artemis 6 is completed, more Artemis missions have been proposed. These missions would focus on expanding the Artemis Base Camp until it becomes permanently occupied. The water ice in the polar craters should provide plenty of drinking water. The water can also be split into oxygen to breathe and hydrogen to power rockets. Lunar dust, rock, and metals found beneath the surface could also be used as building materials for extra base camp modules. Solar panels could capture sunlight for power. Harnessing the resources already on the Moon could help humans colonize other worlds, such as Mars.

Mars is about half the size of Earth.

Concept art of an astronaut on Mars

More than three billion years ago, Mars was a planet a lot like Earth. Mars had water and an atmosphere. Scientists think that it may even have contained simple forms of life. Mars is now dry and barren, but just like the Moon, it contains resources such as water ice that could help humans live there. After living on the Moon, we will know a lot more about making a home on a different world. In this way, the Artemis program is the essential first step in making humans not just Earth creatures but an intergalactic species.

Important Dates

2010	US President Barack Obama announces $58 billion for a new NASA space program to send humans to the Moon and Mars.
2017	Space Policy Directive 1, signed by the White House, enables NASA to work with private companies in its new space program. The program is later named Artemis.
2020	NASA announces that funding to design a new lunar lander for the Artemis program will be provided to private companies.
2021	Private company SpaceX is awarded the contract to supply NASA with a lunar lander, called the Starship Human Landing System. Stacking of Artemis 1 in the Vehicle Assembly Building is completed.
2022	The launch of Artemis 1 is delayed due to technical problems with the rocket. Artemis 1 successfully launches from the Kennedy Space Center in Florida and returns to Earth by splashing down in the Pacific Ocean.

2023 SpaceX's Starship explodes eight minutes into its test flight to reach space and return to Earth.

An audit of the Artemis program estimates its total cost through 2025 will be $93 billion.

2024 After an assessment of the Artemis 1 heat shield failures, NASA announces it will delay the Artemis 2 mission from 2024 to 2025.

SpaceX's Starship successfully blasts into space and orbits Earth but is lost during reentry.

Source Notes

9–10 Jeffrey Kluger, "Why SpaceX's Starship Explosion Is No Big Deal," *Time*, April 20, 2023, https://time.com/6273472/spacex-starship-explosion-no-big-deal/.

11 "President John F. Kennedy Speech to Congress on Space Exploration," The Kennedy Center, accessed January 6, 2025, https://www.kennedy-center.org/video/center/discussionspoken-word/2019/president-john-f.-kennedy-speech-to-congress-on-space-exploration/.

12 Natalie Wolchover, "'One Small Step for Man': Was Neil Armstrong Misquoted?," Space.com, August 27, 2012, https://www.space.com/17307-neil-armstrong-one-small-step-quote.html.

15 Jesse Lee, "21st Century Space Exploration: 'The Next Chapter That We Can Write Together Here at NASA,'" The White House President Barack Obama, April 15, 2010, https://obamawhitehouse.archives.gov/blog/2010/04/15/making-investments-groundbreaking-developments-21st-century-space-exploration.

20 Clare Duffy, "In 2004, Elon Musk Discussed Partnering with NASA for the Next Era of Space Travel. This Weekend Marks a Major Milestone," CNN, May 30, 2020, https://www.cnn.com/2020/05/30/tech/elon-musk-spacex-2004-interview-the-vault/index.html.

22 Claire A. O'Shea, "NASA Selects Blue Origin as Second Artemis Lunar Lander Provider," NASA, May 19, 2023, https://www.nasa.gov/news-release/nasa-selects-blue-origin-as-second-artemis-lunar-lander-provider/.

25 Ashley Strickland, "Today's Artemis I Launch Has Been Scrubbed After Engine Issue," CNN, August 29, 2022, https://www.cnn.com/2022/08/29/world/nasa-artemis-1-launch-scn/index.html.

25 Monisha Ravisetti, "Watch Live: NASA's Artemis I Moon Rocket Launch," CNET, November 15, 2022, https://www.cnet.com/science/space/watch-live-nasas-historic-artemis-i-moon-rocket-launch-tonight/.

30 NASA Office of Inspector General, "NASA's Readiness for the Artemis II Crewed Mission to Lunar Orbit," NASA, May 1, 2024, https://oig.nasa.gov/wp-content/uploads/2024/05/ig-24-011.pdf.

31 Elizabeth Howell, "'It Takes Courage to Make the Right Decision:' Artemis 2 Astronaut Explains Why Moon Mission Was Delayed to 2025," Space.com, February 8, 2024, https://www.space.com/artemis-2-moon-astronaut-delay-support.

35 Mike Wall, "US Must Beat China Back to the Moon, Congress Tells NASA," Space.com, January 17, 2024, https://www.space.com/us-win-moon-race-china-congress-artemis-hearing.

Selected Bibliography

Foust, Jeff. "Starship Lifts Off on Third Test Flight." SpaceNews, March 14, 2024. https://spacenews.com/starship-lifts-off-on-third-test-flight/.

Harvey, Ailsa, and Adam Mann. "NASA's Artemis Program: Everything You Need to Know." Space.com, December 12, 2022. https://www.space.com/artemis-program.html.

Holmes, Oliver. "NASA Postpones Plans to Send Humans to Moon." *Guardian* (US edition), January 10, 2024. https://www.theguardian.com/science/2024/jan/10/nasa-postpones-plans-to-send-humans-to-moon-artemis.

Kluger, Jeffrey. "SpaceX's Starship, the Biggest Rocket Ever Built, Is Poised to Fly." *Time*, April 17, 2023. https://time.com/6252046/spacex-starship-rocket/.

"Space Launch System." NASA. Accessed January 6, 2025. https://www.nasa.gov/reference/space-launch-system/.

Tingley, Brett. "NASA Inspector General Finds Orion Heat Shield Issues 'Pose Significant Risks' to Artemis 2 Crew Safety." Space.com, May 2, 2024. https://www.space.com/nasa-artemis-1-orion-heat-shield-office-inspector-general.

Learn More

Adelman, Beth. *History of Moon Exploration*. Lerner Publications, 2025.

Britannica Kids: Artemis
https://kids.britannica.com/students/article/Artemis/635481

Martin, Claudia. *Earth and the Moon*. Bearport, 2025.

Mooney, Carla. *Christina Hammock Koch: Artemis Astronaut*. Lerner Publications, 2026.

NASA: The Apollo Program
https://www.nasa.gov/the-apollo-program/

NASA: Artemis
https://www.nasa.gov/missions/artemis/

Index

Photo Acknowledgments

Image credits: Dima Zel/Shutterstock, p. 2; Doug Walters/Unsplash, p. 4; Joe Marino/UPI/Alamy, pp. 6, 8, 21; CBW/Alamy, p. 10; MediaPunch Inc/Alamy, p. 11; AP Photo/NASA, pp. 12, 30; NASA, pp. 13, 29, 35–36; S.E.A. Photo/Alamy, p. 14; NASA/Wikimedia Commons, p. 15; AP Photo/Hauke-Christian Dittrich/picture-alliance/dpa, p. 16; NASA/James Schultz, p. 18; AP Photo/Scott Schilke/SipaUSA, p. 19; Soshi Yamada/Getty Images, p. 20; NASA/piemags/Alamy, pp. 23–24; NASA/Getty Images, p. 26; AP Photo/Alex G. Perez/AGPfoto/Sipa USA, p. 27; MARK FELIX/Getty Images, p. 32; ZUMA Press, Inc./Alamy, p. 33; AP Photo/Eric Gay, p. 38; NASA/Bill Ingalls, p. 39; Digital Vision./Getty Images, p. 40; cokada/Getty Images, p. 41. Design elements: Casey Horner/Unsplash; 3d_kot/Shutterstock; Yellow Cloud/Shutterstock.

Cover: NASA/piemags/Alamy.